TABLE OF CONTENTS

FROM A TO Z
WITH BOOKS & ME

Linking Literature With Primary
Self-Concept Programs

by Imogene Forte

Incentive Publications, Inc.
Nashville, Tennessee

Cover and illustrations by Susan Eaddy

ISBN 0-86530-189-1

ABOUT A TO Z WITH ME

FROM A TO Z WITH BOOKS AND ME has been developed to encourage children to think about themselves and the very ordinary things in their lives in a most extraordinary way.

The 26 mini-units are designed to help beginning readers and writers get in touch with, sort out and make meaningful use of their own feelings, ideas and environmental influences.

The activities have been organized in alphabetical sequence to provide a format familiar to the child. This format has been enhanced and made user-friendly by "trigger words" to command attention and stimulate creative self expression.

Beginning with "A is for Almost All About Me" (...the people I know, the places I go and the things I do) through "Z is for Zebra, Zipper and Zoo" (...if I visited the zoo, this is what I would do), children will read, think, draw and write about the people, places and things that make up the wide and wonderful world of which they are a part. Each of the self-concept exploration activities is supported by a carefully adapted literature selection to encourage growth in self-understanding and appreciation of good books. Through this personalized involvement with the high interest skills based activities and correlated book selections, the child's awareness of self and others will take on new and deeper dimensions. The super simple five step instructions (on the next page) will afford quick and easy implementation of the projects in a naturally developmental manner.

HOW TO USE THIS BOOK

1. Turn to pages 66-78 and read the Quick Reference Guide.

2. Thumb through pages 10 to 61 to get the scope and sequence of the activities pages. Match activity pages with the corresponding section of the Quick Reference Guide. In two minutes or less this guide affords a brief synopsis of the literature selection, skills and concepts, and a creative follow-up project. Utilizing the activity pages for motivation and content integration, the book selection for language enrichment and the follow-up as a culminating activity provides a concise, whole language mini-unit with speaking, listening, reading, writing and thinking components.

3. Assemble pencils, crayons, books and activity pages.

4. Help children work through the activity pages in a relaxed and non-threatening setting to allow time for discussion and self expression. (More mature children may be able to complete both pages of a mini-unit in one session, while others will need two). Time and freedom to ponder and process spontaneous reactions and responses is of the utmost importance. As motivation for the project present the first mini-unit (Almost All About Me) and discuss the concept of "A to Z With Books and Me" and the fact that the completed activity pages will become a personal record of impressions, thoughts and feelings.

5. As a culminating activity, the booklet cover (page 9) may be completed, added to the activity pages and bound (by hole punch and tying with ribbon or yarn) to make a one of a kind "All About Me" book, sure to be treasured for years to come.

This Book Belongs to

_____

A is for Almost All ABOUT Me

My name is:_____

Here I am!

All About Me

This book is about...
the people I know
the places I go
and the things I do.
Here they are!

people

places

things

B is for Butterflies, Birthdays, and BOOKS

Write the name of a favorite book on each band of the rainbow.

The rainbow colors are blue, indigo, violet, green, yellow, orange, and red.

Color your rainbow.

My Favorite Book

The name of my very favorite book is _____

_____

The author's name is _____

Here is a picture of the part of the book I like best.

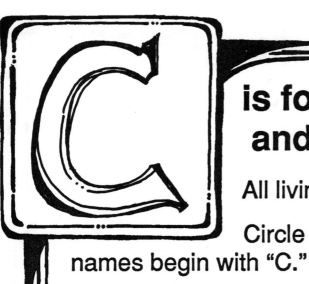

is for Clocks, Calendars, and CHANGES

All living things grow and change.

Circle pictures of 4 living things whose names begin with "C."

Make an X on pictures of 7 nonliving things whose names begin with "C."

Changes, Changes

All living things grow and change.

All living things need food, air, and water to live.

I am a living thing.

I am growing and changing.

I am _____ years old.

I am _____ feet and _____ inches tall.

I weigh _____ pounds.

I weigh _____ pounds more than I did last year.

My hair is _____ than it was last year.

Two things that have changed about me during the last two years are:

1. _____

2. _____

Two things about me that have not changed in the last two years are:

1. _____

2. _____

One thing about me that I hope will change before next year is _____ .

Every day, I grow and change.

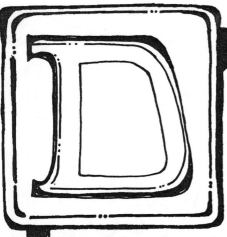

D is for Dinosaurs, Dragons, and DREAMS

Pretend that on a lazy summer day, you are lying on your back looking at the clouds.

You fall asleep to dream of meeting a dragon and a dinosaur in your own backyard. Draw your dream.

A Dream To Keep

There are all kinds of dreams.

Dreams can be dangerous, daring, delightful, doubtful, disgusting, dreadful, or delicious.

Some of the best dreams of all are daydreams – the ones you make up when you are wide awake and just put together the thoughts in your head about something you would like to do and how you would do it.

Draw a picture of one of your daydreams.

E is for Eyes, Ears, and the EARTH

Earth Watch

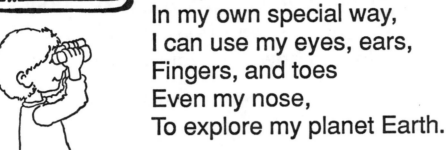

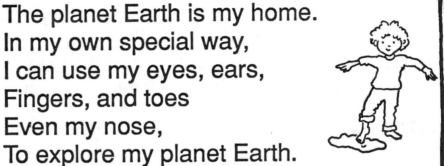

The planet Earth is my home.
In my own special way,
I can use my eyes, ears,
Fingers, and toes
Even my nose,
To explore my planet Earth.

Here are some things I can do to make the Earth a better place to live.

Pollution Solution

Find and circle 8 causes of pollution. Can you think of a pollution solution for your neighborhood?

F

is for Faces, Families, & FRIENDS

Here I am with two friends.

FRIENDLY PORTRAIT

A Friendly Sandwich

If I had a giant sandwich,
Some cookies and milk and a game,
I'd share them all with my best friend...

_____ is my best friend's name.

And after we'd finished eating,
And had played for a while,
Here are some of the things
We'd do to make us smile!

G is for Grand, Glorious, & GROWNUPS

Sometimes it's hard for grownups
and kids to understand each other

Each wonders why the other does
some of the things they do

And each wishes the other knew.

Here is something I do that grownups don't understand.

Here is something grownups do that I don't understand.

When I Am A Grownup

Here is something that I am not allowed to do now that I look forward to doing when I am a grownup.

is for **Habits, Hugs, &**
HOMES

Home may be a house, a castle, a cabin, just a room, or even a boat.

Wherever a family lives, they add their own special touches to make it home.

Draw and color doors, windows, and other special touches to turn this house into a home.

Make up a story about the family who would live here.

Home Sweet Home

One thing I would change
about my home...

The thing I like best
about my home...

Here is something I could do to make my home a
nicer place to live.

I

is for Insects, Imagination, & ICE CREAM

List the names of 2 people you would invite to an ice cream party.

1. _____

2. _____

Show the ice cream treat you think each person would like best.

Person	Ice Cream Treat
1.	
2.	

To find out how well you really know your friends, check with them to see if you chose correctly.

Ice Cream Cones and Imagination

Thinking of new ways to use ordinary things helps stretch your imagination and makes you "extraordinary."

Show 2 ways to use an ice cream cone for something other than holding ice cream.

Connect the dots from 1 to 25 to frame your work.

J is for Jingles, Jump Ropes, & JOBS

Whatever Shall I Be?

When I grow up, I'd like to be
The captain of a ship at sea,
Or pilot jets to far away
And bring them back another day.

Perhaps I'd rather tell the news
And do important interviews,
Write songs or books or poems or plays
Or dance in beautiful ballets.

I could be a detective who catches thieves
Or a gardener fine who rakes great piles of leaves,
A plumber, a drummer, a daring sky diver,
A mayor, bricklayer, or taxicab driver...

An astronaut brave who rockets so high
Or a master chef who is known for his pie
A florist, a seamstress, a doctor, a farmer,
A basketball player, or a famous snake charmer.

How will I decide just what I will be?
There are so many jobs...which one is for me?
Someday I will know, and I'll choose my own.
But today I'll just dream what I'll be when I'm grown.

On The Job

Find and color pictures of 10 workers in this scene.
Circle the job you think would be the most fun.

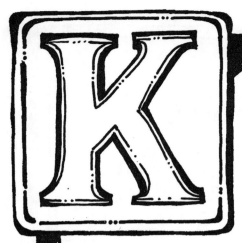  **is for Kittens, Kisses,
&
KITCHENS**

Kitchens are for kids!

Here is a meal I can fix without help.

My favorite food in all the world is _____ .

A Kitchen Mess

Tidy up this kitchen!

Some, but not all, of these things belong here.

Circle the things you might use to make a meal.

Draw a line to the basket from each of the things that don't belong in the kitchen.

Draw yourself in the picture making your favorite food.

L is for Loving, Laughing, & LISTENING

The world is full of sounds.
Some make us feel good.
Some make us feel bad.
Some we don't even hear.

List 3 scary sounds.

1. _____
2. _____
3. _____

List 3 sad sounds.

1. _____
2. _____
3. _____

List 3 happy sounds.

1. _____
2. _____
3. _____

Listening and Feeling

Here is a black, blue, and purple scribble drawing to show how I feel when I listen to stormy sounds in the middle of the night.

Here is a pink, red, and yellow drawing to show how I feel when I listen to birds singing on a beautiful spring day.

M is for Magic, Mystery, and MAKE-BELIEVE

Elves and gnomes and leprechauns
Are fluttery fairy folks
Full of mystery and magic,
Make-believe and jokes.

If they gave me a magic carpet
To carry me to and fro,
This is what I'd do,
and here is where I'd go.

Make-Believe

Remember the story of Alladin and his magic lamp? Whenever Alladin wanted something, all he had to do was rub his lamp and a genie would appear to grant his wish.

Pretend you own a magic lamp.

Write or draw the one thing you would wish for more than anything else in the whole world.

N is for Neighbors, Numbers, & NAMES

I can write my name backward.

_____

I can write my name upside down.

_____

I can write my name round
and round in a circle.

The important thing about
my name is that it's all mine.
Anytime, anywhere, any way I write my name,
it belongs to me, and it tells you who I am.

Speaking of Names

Here are some of my VIP names.

a person who
makes me laugh

a person I like
to eat lunch with

a person who
cooks food I like

a fine teacher

And here is a picture of a very important person in
my life.

is for Octopus, Oysters, and OPINIONS

Select one of these statements,
and tell why you think it is true.
- In my opinion, every kid should have
  a pet.
- In my opinion, kids don't need pets.

_____

_____

_____

_____

In My Opinion

Look up the word "opinion" in the dictionary to make sure you know its real meaning.

People have such strong opinions about things that it is easy to confuse fact and opinion.

Read the paragraph about octopuses. Underline 3 facts, and circle 3 opinions.

Complete the paragraph with one opinion of your own.

Octopuses are mollusks. They are ugly animals. They feed mainly on crabs and lobsters. Sometimes they may eject a cloud of ink when alarmed. Children hate octopuses. No one would care if all the octopuses in the world disappeared.

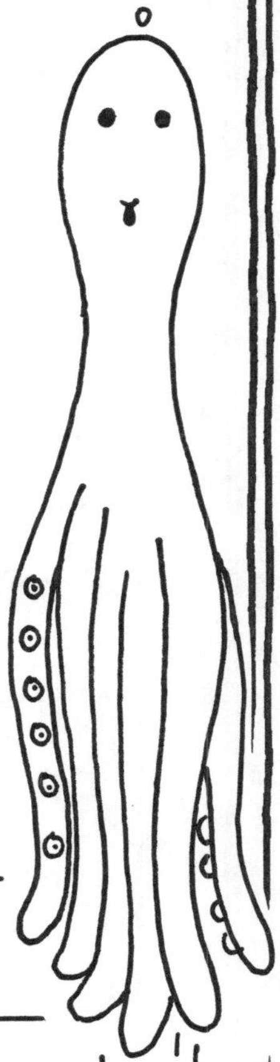

_____

_____

_____

_____

_____

P is for People, Privacy, & PLACES

Far Away and Close to Home

These special places, I call my own.

A place of my dreams

A place to be alone

A fun "people place" to be with others.

A learning place

Places To Go and Things To Do

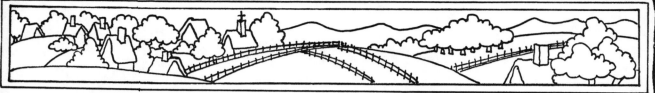

If only I could, this is where I would go
And this is what I would do.

Next Sunday with my family I would go _____

   and we would _____ .

After school on Monday I would go _____

   and I would _____ .

Every Tuesday for a month I would go _____

   so that I could _____ .

Some Wednesday next summer I would go _____

   and when I got there I would _____ .

With my class on Thursday, I would go on a

   field trip to _____

   to learn about _____ .

Friday night I would like to go _____

   because _____ .

On Saturday with two friends I would go _____

   and we would _____

   _____ .

Q

is for Quilt, Quiet, & QUESTION

Do you remember the story of the old man and his wife who wasted their three wishes because they wished before they thought?

Sometimes we waste questions the very same way – we ask questions before we think about what we really want to know.

Write three questions that you would like to have answers for.

1. _____

_____

2. _____

_____

3. _____

_____

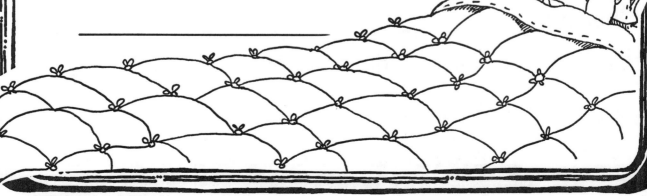

Quick Questions

Quick!

Draw answers for these quick questions.

How does it feel
 to be called a
 quitter?

What do you like
 to do in your
 "quiet time"?

What would you
 do first if you
 were queen or
 king for a day?

Write a "quick question" you would like to ask
 your teacher.

R is for Reading, Rainbows, & RELATIVES

Relatives come in all ages, shapes, and sizes.

There is something special about each and every one.

Altogether, they make a family that is one of a kind.

Use markers or crayons to add words and pictures to make this family coat of arms show the things that make your family special.

Special Relatives

There is something special about each of my relatives.

The relative that I need when I am sad is _____.

The relative that I like to play with is _____ .

The relative who needs me the most is _____ .

The relative I would like to take a trip with is

_____.

The relative who makes me laugh most often is

_____.

S is for Sunshine, Shadows, & SEASONS

Seasons come and seasons go,
Winter, summer, spring, and fall.
Here on this poster, I will show
The season I like best of all!

Seasonal Holidays

Every season brings its own special holidays.

Fill the Holiday Go-Round with words and pictures to show your special holidays.

Make a star beside your very favorite holiday.

T is for Trips, Trust, & TIME

Draw pictures on the clockface to show how you spend your time each day.

Begin with getting up, and end with going to bed again.

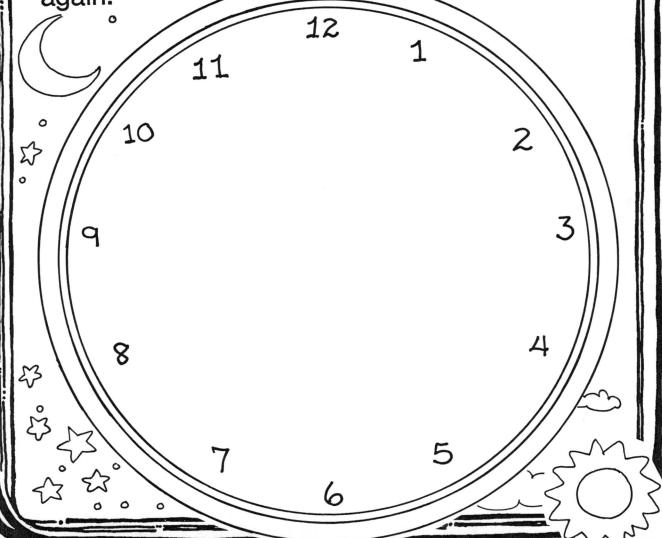

Time Capsule

Design a time capsule to be opened ten years from now to tell people about the world today.

Include items that reflect your community, country, environment, and you.

Time Capsule of _____ Date _____

2007 • 2008 • 2009 • ⬭ • 2010 • 2011 • 2012 •

2001 • 2002 • 2003 • ⬭ • 2004 • 2005 • 2006

U is for Unicorns, Umbrellas, & UNIQUE

Unique means being the only one of a kind.

I am unique!

There is not one single person in the whole world exactly like me.

Three things that make me uniquely me are:

1._____

2._____

3._____

Of all the things about me that make me unique, I'm most proud of:

_____

_____

_____

One of a Kind

Some people like popcorn.
Others hate peanuts.
One person even likes
 soup a la coconuts!

My favorite treat is

_____

But I just despise

_____

NEVER

Some people like baseball.
Some people won't swim.
Some people like tennis.
Some people hate gym.

My favorite sport is _____

But I hate to play _____

Some people like hot weather.
Others like snow.
And some like rainy days
Wherever they go.

My favorite weather is

_____

But I just hate it when it

_____

V is for Vegetables, Violets, & VERY WELL

Use your favorite color crayon to check the box that shows how well you can do each of the things listed.

When you have finished, ask a friend to use a different color to do the same thing.

Compare the checks.

I Can	Not Well/ Not At All	Pretty Well	Very Well
sew			
cook			
read			
write			
spell			
swim			
dance			
sing			
whistle			
draw			

Isn't it wonderful that people are different and can do different things well?

Very Well

Fill this valuable "V" with pictures of things you do very well.

Something I do very well that I could not do at all last year.

Something I do very well now and hope to do better next year.

Something I do very well at school.

W is for Wishes, Windows, & the WORLD

Every window frames a picture of the world outside.

What kind of picture does your window frame?

Pretend you are an artist and draw the picture.

A Big, Wide Wonderful World

I am a part of a great big,
wonderful world.
In this wonderful, enormous world
What's a child to do
But go exploring and adventuring,
Discovering what is new...
Listening to the sounds of night,
Making friends with rain,
Catching hands with the best of pals
And racing down the lane.
Learning fields and roads and places
Where a kid would love to roam,
Finding jobs to do and folks to know,
Feeling good at home.

I am part of
something
BIG!

HERE I AM

 From FROM HERE TO THE EDGE OF THE WORLD, © 1978 by Incentive Publications, Inc., Nashville, TN.
Used with permission.

X is for "X marks the spot," Xylophone,

and X RAY

X rays show parts of the body which can't be seen from the outside.

Here is a list of body parts you have that you can't see.

Draw a line from each one to where you think it would show up in an X ray.

- heart
- lungs
- kidneys
- backbone
- pelvis
- jawbone
- shoulder bone
- knee bone
- brain

X ray View

Read each sentence below, and decide whether it is true or false.
Circle the letter in the correct column to find out how the doctor sees your body with an X ray.

	True	False
1. Your heart is in your stomach.	A	I
2. Most people have two knees.	N	W
3. Good eating habits build strong bodies.	S	E
4. Your lungs are right above your feet.	G	I
5. People normally have ten toes and ten fingers.	D	O
6. Your jawbone helps you walk.	F	E
7. Your brain is where you do your thinking.	O	S
8. Your backbone is part of your arm.	B	U
9. Your elbow is where your arm bends.	T	C

Now copy the circled letters here to find out how "body wise" you are.

___ ___ ___ ___ ___ ___ ___ ___ ___
1   2   3   4   5   6   7   8   9

Y

is for You, Yak, & YAWN

I yawn when I am bored.
I become bored when _____

_____

But I stop yawning and wake up when _____

_____

I think my teacher yawns when _____

_____

Sometimes I yawn just because I am sleepy, tired, and it is time for bed.

The Sad Story of Yannie Yawn

Yannie Yawn loves to stay up late at night. After everyone else is in bed, he turns on the television to watch the late, late show and stuffs himself with chocolate cake, potato chips, and strawberry pop. He also forgets to take his bath and brush his teeth.

He simply cannot stop yawning. Yannie yawns at the breakfast table, in the classroom, and on the playground. Why, Yannie even yawns at the circus and would you believe at his own birthday party!

Yannie really needs some good advice. If he were my friend, I would tell him he needs to: _____

_____

_____

My Own Bedtime Habits

I would rate my own bedtime habits as:

_____ Good

_____ Not So Good

_____ Pretty Good

This morning I got up at _____

Last night I went to bed at _____

I need to _____

_____

Z is for Zebra, Zipper, & ZOO

Running a zoo could be fun, but it would be a big job, too. Pretend you are a zookeeper for a day. List your duties.

1._____

2._____

3._____

List the good points of the job.

1._____

2._____

List the bad points of the job.

1._____

2._____

On another sheet of paper, draw a picture to show the thing you would enjoy most about the job.

A Visit to the Zoo

Animals like people come in all shapes,
sizes, colors, and even personalities.
If I visited the zoo, here is what I would do!

To make me laugh
I would watch the

_____

I would study
the habits of
the long-necked

_____

I would watch the

_____

swing their trunks to
and fro.

I would listen to the roar of the

_____

BOOKMARKS

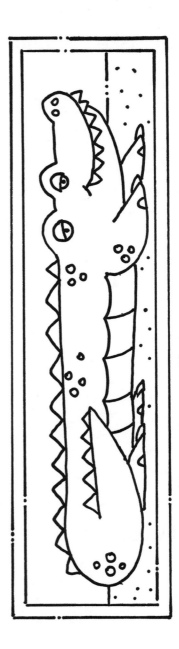

MY READING RECORD

RATING SCALE	
GOOD	☆
FAIR	O
POOR	X

DATE	TITLE OF BOOK	NEW WORDS	PAGES READ	RATING

A to Z
Word List

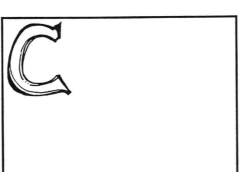

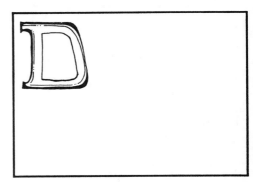

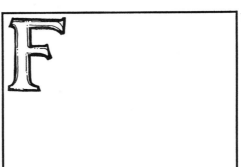

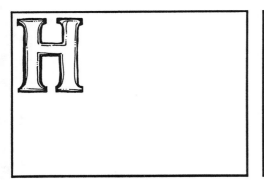

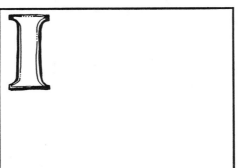

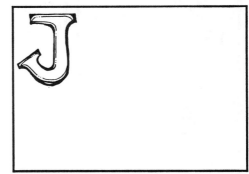

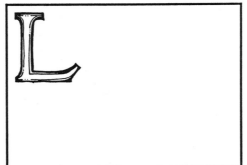

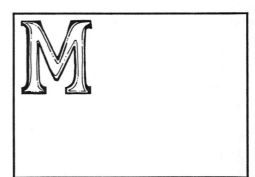

A to Z
Word List

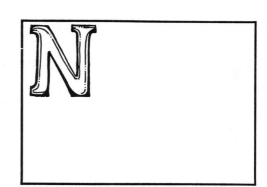

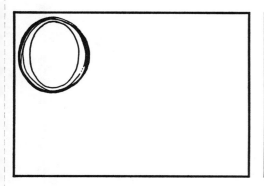

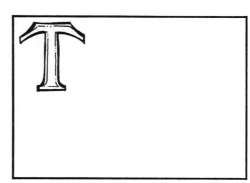

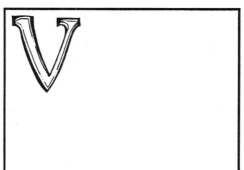

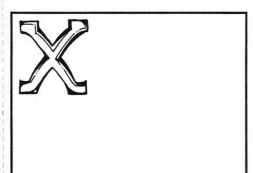

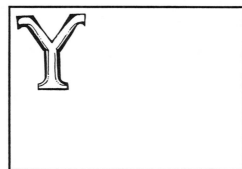

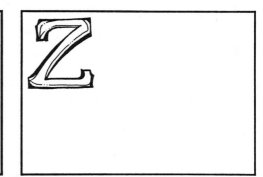

Quick Reference Guide

is for Almost, All, and About Me
Literature Connection: *Dandelion*

Summary: A lovable lion overdoes his attempt to be grand and is not recognized by the hostess who invited him to the big party. It's only after a stormy experience that he learns that it is just fine to be "plain me."

Curriculum Integration: Social studies, language, art

Concept Exploration: People, places, things, and self-awareness

Skills: Creative thinking, drawing, handwriting

Follow-up: Cut pictures and words from old magazines to paste on a shoe box to make a "me box." Fill the shoe box with special things.

is for Butterflies, Birthdays, and Books
Literature Connection: *Check It Out*

Summary: Libraries, too, come in all shapes, sizes, and styles. From the Library of Congress to school libraries, this book about libraries explains and gives instructions for using the riches to be found in libraries.

Curriculum Integration: Language

Concept Exploration: Book preferences

Skills: Valuing, decision-making, recordkeeping

Follow-up: Use construction paper and art supplies to make bookmarks to celebrate the love of books. Plan a special book lovers party for each person to bring a book to tell about or share in some creative way. Use the bookmarks for favors.

is for Clocks, Calendars, and Changes

Literature Connection: *A Color of His Own*

Summary: The little chameleon is sad because he has no color of his own. He worries until he meets an older and wiser chameleon who solves the problem by giving him someone he can always be "just like."

Curriculum Integration: Science, social studies, math, language

Concept Exploration: Living and nonliving things, body and environmental awareness

Skills: Visual discrimination, categorizing, counting, reading, writing, observing

Follow-up: Grow a windowsill garden. Rest a sweet potato on toothpicks in a jar of water. Put carrot tops in a shallow dish. Place a pineapple top in a pan of water. Plant an avocado seed in a pot of soil. Plant parsley seeds on a damp sponge. Place in a sunny window and watch your garden grow!

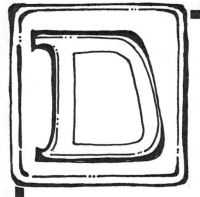

is for Dinosaurs, Dragons, and Dreams

Literature Connection: *Where the Wild Things Are*

Summary: A little boy in the privacy of his own bedroom creates a fantasy world inhabited by the most imaginative monsters possible. Fortunately, the adventures are more friendly than frightening.

Curriculum Integration: Language, social studies

Concept Exploration: Imagination, fantasy, self-awareness, futurism

Skills: Creative thinking, developing plot and sequence, writing

Follow-up: Read or tell the story of Rip Van Winkle who fell asleep to wake up years later to find that many changes had taken place while he slept. Discuss and list the changes a person who had fallen asleep 100 or even 10 years ago would find in the world today.

is for Eyes, Ears, and Earth

Literature Connection: *Little Fox Goes to the End of the Earth*

Summary: While Little Fox unfolds the story of the daring journey she will take to the end of the earth, her mother sews a coat for her to wear.

Curriculum Integration: Science, social studies, language

Concept Exploration: Environmental, ecological, and social awareness

Skills: Reading, visual discrimination, visualizing, valuing

Follow-up: Use construction paper and art supplies to make earth celebration posters to encourage people to take good care of our planet earth.

is for Faces, Families, and Friends

Literature Connection: *Frog and Toad Together*

Summary: Five individual stories illustrate how Frog and Toad's loyal and sharing friendship conquers everyday experiences of disappointment, impatience, fear, need for recognition, lack of willpower, and loneliness.

Curriculum Integration: Language, social studies, art

Concept Exploration: Friendship, valuing, self-awareness

Skills: Evaluative thinking, drawing, listing

Follow-up: List qualities important to friendship and activities that friends enjoy doing together. Draw or paint a mural of friends doing things together that demonstrate the qualities of friendship.

Poetry Bonus: Share and enjoy *Are You My Friend Today* by Gyo Fujikawa, Random House, 1988.

is for Grand, Glorious, and Grownups

Literary Connection: *Sea Swan*

Summary: After Mrs. Swan's grandchildren's visit, she remembers good times they had and begins to think of things she never learned to do that might be fun. The events that follow change her life and help her gain new self-respect.

Curriculum Integration: Social studies, language

Concept Exploration: Self-awareness, futurism

Skills: Brainstorming, synthesizing, creative expression, interviewing

Follow-up: Interview grownups to find out what they looked forward to doing as grownups when they were younger. Ask if they have achieved their goals and what factors contributed to the outcome.

is for Habits, Hugs, and Homes

Literature Connection: *The Biggest House in the World*

Summary: A wise father snail tells his son, who wants to grow up to have the biggest house in the world, a story. After hearing about a little snail who did indeed discover how to make his house grow and grow but came to no good end, the little snail decides that his own house is just right as it is.

Curriculum Integration: Social studies, language

Concept Exploration: Homes, families, and self-awareness

Skills: Analytical thinking, drawing, listing, brainstorming

Follow-up: List different kinds of homes. Try to write the name of a family who lives in each type of home listed. Begin with a high-rise apartment, motor home, boat, log cabin, castle, mansion, two-story, ranch style, farm house, etc. Add as many as you can think of. Use fictional, celebrity, and TV families as well as ones you know. Discuss the differences in life-styles.

is for Insects, Imagination, & Ice Cream

Literature Connection: *Ice Cream Soup*

Summary: Marvin and Milton are friends and decide to give a party and make everything themselves. Even though they work hard, they learn that not everything is as easy as it appears. Friends surprise them with their help.

Curriculum Integration: Math, social studies, language

Concept Exploration: Individuality, personal preferences, friendship

Skills: Problem-solving, numerical order, designing

Follow-up: Use available art supplies to concoct imaginary ice cream treats. If possible, visit an ice cream store and count the different flavors and toppings available.

is for Jingles, Jump Ropes, and Jobs

Literature Connection: *The Berenstain Bears On the Job*

Summary: Two young bears think of all the things they could be when they grow up. From firefighter to farmer, they weigh the pros and cons but decide not to fret for yet awhile.

Curriculum Integration: Social studies, language/poetry

Concept Exploration: The world of work, career and self-awareness

Skills: Reading, visual discrimination, evaluating

Follow-up: List family members and their jobs. Interview each person to find out what traits, abilities, and training were required. Ask also what the good and bad points of their jobs are, and list these beside each job.

K is for Kittens, Kisses, and Kitchens

Literature Connection: *Strega Nona*

Summary: Big Anthony is tempted to show off Strega Nona's magic pasta pot. His untrustworthiness is rewarded by a punishment to fit the crime and a stomachache.

Curriculum Integration: Health, art, math, language, science

Concept Exploration: Homes, food, tools, self-awareness

Skills: Decision-making, drawing, categorization, reading directions, measuring

Follow-up: Follow the package directions to cook a pot of pasta. Use the stated measurement per person to compute the amount of pasta, salt, and water necessary for the number of people to be fed. Season the pasta with butter and parmesan cheese or a canned tomato sauce. Add bread, green salad, fruit, and milk for a perfectly balanced meal.

Discussion Bonus: What makes the cooked pasta expand to more than twice its uncooked volume?

L is for Loving, Laughing, and Listening

Literature Connection: *Shhhhhh...Bang, a Whispering Book*

Summary: A little boy arrives in a town where everyone whispers. He makes a lot of noise to gain attention. As the people in the town wake up and begin to talk again, the story ends happily for all.

Curriculum Integration: Science, language, social studies

Concept Exploration: Environmental and emotional awareness, feelings

Skills: Visualizing, drawing, listing

Follow-up: Read and enjoy some other "noisy" books by Margaret Wise Brown. Then take a listening walk and draw a picture to show all the sounds heard.

(*Noisy Book, Country Noisy Book, Summer Noisy Book, Inside Noisy Book, Quiet Noisy Book, Winter Noisy Book*)

is for Mystery, Magic, and Make-Believe

Literature Connection: *Humbug Witch*

Summary: A frightening-looking, horrible, witchey witch with a good sturdy broom and a cat named Fred try to perform some extraordinary magic. When even her magic brew fails and none of her magic tricks work, she just goes off to bed – as does Fred.

Curriculum Integration: Language, social studies

Concept Exploration: Self-understanding

Skills: Brainstorming, refining, self-expression, drama

Follow-up: Use dress-up clothes (hats, shoes, gloves, etc.), makeup, and props to impersonate make-believe characters such as a gnome, witch, troll, elf, ghost, giant, leprechaun, etc. Invent a name, personality, place of residence, and a scenario with an intended purpose. For example, Ellie the elf who lives in the back hall closet wants to trick the cook into baking a cheesecake to celebrate the birthday of the mouse who also lives in Ellie's closet. Act out the scenarios and be sure to provide a happy ending.

is for Neighbors, Numbers, and Names

Literature Connection: *Wilfrid Gordon McDonald Partridge*

Summary: A young boy with a very long name seeks advice from a number of elderly citizens to enable him to help a friend with another very long name solve a problem. Sharing objects and memories helps Miss Nancy regain her memory.

Curriculum Integration: Social studies, language

Concept Exploration: Friendship, aging, environmental and self-awareness

Skills: Handwriting, valuing, drawing

Follow-up: Make The Name is a Game lists. For each letter of the alphabet, try to list the name of an animal, a plant, and a mineral. Use the completed list to play, "plant, animal, or mineral game." The first player says, "I'm thinking of something that begins with an 'A.'" Then this person gives 3 clues. Then the other player guesses.

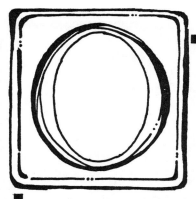

is for Octopuses, Oysters, and Opinions

Literature Connection: *If I Ran The Zoo*

Summary: Young Gerald McCrew has very strong opinions about what he would do if he ran the zoo. The search for imaginative beasts of a most unusual kind to replace the present animals that he sees as "not quite good enough" provides a fun romp through faraway places and presents some most unusual faces.

Curriculum Integration: Social studies, language, science

Concept Exploration: Environmental and self-awareness.

Skills: Distinguishing fact and opinion, interviewing, charting, reading, analytical thinking

Follow-up: Read and discuss the advertisements in last Sunday's newspaper to determine how many are based on fact and how many on opinion. Write creative ads based on fact or opinion.

is for People, Privacy, and Places

Literature Connection: *Hey, Al*

Summary: Al, a janitor, and his dog Eddie live modestly in a single room until a mysterious bird transports them to an island paradise in the sky. All goes well until some strange happenings convince them to flee the life of luxury and come to the conclusion that home is, after all, the best place to be.

Curriculum Integration: Science, social studies, language

Concept Exploration: Days of the week, environmental and self-awareness

Skills: Analytical thinking, sentence structure, writing

Follow-up: Use a world map to locate a jungle place, desert place, a seaside place, a mountain place, a place where it is hot most of the time, a place where it is cold most of the time, and other places of interest. Discuss special features of each place.

is for Quilt, Quiet, and Question

Literature Connection: *Sylvester and the Magic Pebble*

Summary: Sylvester finds a pebble that works magic as long as he holds it in his hand. He turns himself into a rock to escape a lion and drops the pebble. Sylvester and his family are sad until they are reunited and realize that they have all they need without using magic.

Curriculum Integration: Language, social studies

Concept Exploration: Feelings, self-awareness, relationships

Skills: Questioning, refining, decision-making, valuing

Follow-up: Make a list of questions about topics of interest such as food, animals, community helpers, weather, plants, etc. Find and write answers to the questions and use the two lists to play question and answer games based on games such as Trivial Pursuit®, Pictograph, or Twenty Questions. If you are really ambitious, design, make, and play an original board game using the two lists.

is for Reading, Rainbows, and Relatives

Literature Connection: *The Relatives Came*

Summary: When the relatives of all ages arrive in a big station wagon overloaded with food, luggage, and other assorted goodies, the fun begins. Hugs and kisses, laughing, music, talking, and sharing make this a memorable visit worth repeating.

Curriculum Integration: Social studies, language

Concept Exploration: Families, relationships, personal preferences

Skills: Visualizing, researching, organizing, information, drawing, writing

Follow-up: Make name and address books including relatives far and near. Research locations and write and mail letters or greeting cards to the relative who lives the furthest away and to the youngest and oldest relatives.

is for Sunshine, Shadows, and Seasons

Literature Connection: *I Know a Lady*

Summary: A delightful neighbor works in her garden, calls greetings, and gives away flowers, candy apples, cookies, sodas, and more. As the seasons come and go, her smiles and treats warm the hearts of boys and girls.

Curriculum Integration: Social studies, science, language, math

Concept Exploration: Seasons, weather, holidays, and self-awareness

Skills: Valuing, vocabulary usage, writing and drawing, reading a thermometer

Follow-up: Discuss the weather for each season. Learn to read a thermometer and keep a temperature record for a few days just to get practice being a weather forecaster.

is for Trips, Trust, and Time

Literature Connection: *The Guy Who was Five Minutes Late*

Summary: Born five minutes late, this boy continues to be five minutes behind for every event in his life. Luckily he finally meets a princess who shares his plight and they happily wed.

Curriculum Integration: Language, social studies, art

Concept Exploration: Environmental and self-awareness, futurism, time

Skills: Valuing, analytical thinking, creative self-expression, visualizing

Follow-up: On a large sheet of paper, draw pictures of every kind of clock you can think of: cuckoo clock, grandfather clock, clock radio, travel clock, alarm clock, digital clock, etc. Use the picture for a scavenger hunt. Check each clock off as it is located. The first person to find all the clocks is declared the winner.

is for Unicorns, Umbrellas, and Unique

Literature Connection: *Old Henry*

Summary: When Old Henry moves into a neglected house and continues to ignore its upkeep, the neighbors become concerned. It's only after he moved away that both the neighbors and Old Henry decide maybe a compromise could be reached.

Curriculum Integration: Social studies, language

Concept Exploration: Uniqueness of individuals, physical awareness, personal preferences

Skills: Evaluating, decision-making, word usage, visualizing

Follow-up: Write a paragraph or draw a picture to show one thing that is unique about your teacher.

is for Violins, Violets, and Very Well

Literature Connection: *Harry's Song*

Summary: In fall as the other animals prepare for winter, Harry Rabbit continues to do something he does very well – just sit and sing. When winter comes, it is Harry, a one-of-a-kind rabbit, who delights his mother with his contribution of a perfect summer day song to carry the family through the winter.

Curriculum Integration: Social studies, language, art

Concept Exploration: Talents and abilities, expectations, achievements, differences

Skills: Comparing/contrasting, evaluating, charting, drawing, letter writing

Follow-up: Write thank-you letters to people who do their own thing very well to make life more pleasant at home, school, and in the community. Mail the letters.

is for Wishes, Windows, and the World

Literature Connection: *People*

Summary: Detailed illustrations reinforce concise textual portrayal of people around the world. The differences of the 4 billion people in the world are celebrated in a manner that instills pride in the uniqueness of each person.

Curriculum Integration: Social studies, language, art

Concept Exploration: The world and its people

Skills: Visualizing, synthesizing, drawing, understanding poetry, interpreting

Follow-up: Select a country to research whose life-styles are very different from your own. Write a description of the way of life there including: homes, food, clothing, jobs, holidays, habits, etc. Draw and cut out 2 identical, large paper dolls. Draw facial features, hair, clothes, and other details to make one paper doll represent you. Draw the features on the other to represent a child living in the country you researched.

is for "X marks the spot," Xylophone, and X Ray

Literature Connection: *Funnybones*

Summary: One big skeleton, one little skeleton, and their dog skeleton take a walk, play in the park, and meet other skeletons in the zoo. When they can find no one to frighten, they enjoy frightening one another.

Curriculum Integration: Science, social studies, language

Concept Exploration: Body awareness

Skills: Body parts identification, deductive thinking, visualizing, vocabulary extension

Follow-up: Play an X Ray vision game to "see" what is in the mind. One player selects an item in the room, gives hints about it and asks other players to name the item. The object of the game is to give the most creative hints possible to stretch imaginations and stimulate lively dialogue.

Y is for You, Yak, and Yawn
Literature Connection: *Good Night Moon*

Summary: In few words and delightful pictures, a little bunny says good-night to all the objects in the house. Just before he drops off to sleep, he says good-night to the old lady whispering "hush," to the moon, stars, even the air and noises everywhere.

Curriculum Integration: Science, language, social studies

Concept Exploration: Health, bedtime, boredom, self-awareness

Skills: Reading, narrative writing, problem-solving, rating

Follow-up: Paint crayon resist nighttime/bedtime pictures. Use wax crayons to draw bedtime/nighttime scenes. Brush over the entire drawing with a very thin black or dark blue tempera paint wash.

Z is for Zebra, Zipper, and Zoo
Literature Connection: *May I Bring A Friend*

Summary: When an invitation for tea with the king and queen comes, an initiative boy asks permission to bring a friend. As other invitations follow, more friends come also until Saturday when the tables are turned and all the friends share tea at the zoo.

Curriculum Integration: Social studies, language, art

Concept Exploration: Animal characteristics, environmental and self-awareness

Skills: Answering questions, drawing, listing, word usage

Follow-up: Make a list of words that rhyme with "zoo." Use the rhyming words to write short humorous poems about the zoo.

BIBLIOGRAPHY

Alfrid Gordon McDonald Partridge, Mem Fox, illustrated by Julie Vivas. Kan—Midler, 1985.

The Berenstain Bears On the Job, Stan and Jan Berenstain. Random House, 1987.

The Biggest House in the World, written and illustrated by Leo Lionni. Partheon, 1968.

Check It Out, written and illustrated by Gail Gibbons. Harcourt, 1985.

A Color of His Own, written and illustrated by Leo Lionni. Pantheon, 1975.

Dandelion, story and pictures Don Freeman. Puffin Books, 1964.

Frog and Toad Together, Arnold Lobel. Harper and Row, 1972.

Funnybones, Janet and Allan Ahlberg. Scholastic, Inc.; 1980.

Good Night Moon, Margaret Wise Brown, illustrated by Clement Hurd. Harper and Row, 1974.

The Guy Who was Five Minutes Late, William G. Grossman, illustrated by Judy Glasser. Harper and Row, 1990.

Harry's Song, written and illustrated by Lillian Hoban. Greenwillow, 1980.

Hey, Al; Arthur Yorinks; illustrated by Richard Egielski. Farrar, Straus and Giroux; 1986.

Humbug Witch, written and illustrated by Lorna Ballian. Abingdon Press, 1965.

I Know A Lady, Charlotte Zolotow, illustrated by James Stevenson. Greenwillow, 1984.

Ice Cream Soup, Frank Modell. Greenwillow Books, 1988.

If I Ran The Zoo, written and illustrated by Dr. Seuss. Random House, 1977.

Little Fox Goes to the End of the Earth, Ann Tompert, illustrated by John Wallner. Crown, 1976.

May I Bring A Friend, Beatrice de Regniers, illustrated by Beni Montressor. Antheneum, 1969.

Old Henry, by Joan W. Blow, illustrated by Stephen Gammel. Morrow, 1987.

People, written and illustrated by Peter Spier. Doubleday, 1980.

The Relatives Came, Cynthia Rylant, illustrated by Stephen Gammell. Bradbury Press, 1985.

Sea Swan, Kathryn Lasky, illustrated by Catherine Stack. MacMillan, 1988.

Shhhhhh...Bang, a Whispering Book, Margaret Wise Brown, illustrated by Robert De Veyrac. Harper and Row, 1943.

Strega Nona, retold and illustrated by Tomie de Paola. Prentice Hall, 1975.

Sylvester and the Magic Pebble, William Steig. Windmill Books, 1970.

Where the Wild Things Are, written and illustrated by Maurice Sendak. Harper and Row, 1963.